Surviving With Beans And Rice

A Prepper's Cookbook

JM Mason

Survival Zulu, LLC is on a mission to help people become more self reliant.

Surviving With Beans And Rice: A Prepper's Cookbook
by JM Mason
1st Edition, Paperback
Published by Survival Zulu, LLC
www.survivalzulu.com

Copyright © 2022 JM Mason

All rights reserved. No part of this publication may be reproduced, distributed, or transmitted in any form or by any means, including, but not limited to, photocopying, recording, or other electronic or mechanical methods, without the prior written permission of the publisher, except in the case of brief quotations embodied in critical reviews and certain other noncommercial uses permitted by copyright law. For permission requests, you can contact the publisher at www.survivalzulu.com .

Book Cover Design by JM Mason

Contents

Introduction 1

Storage 4

Equivalents 6

Main Dishes

    Classic Red Beans and Rice 10
    Spanish Beans and Rice 12
    Taco Beans and Rice 14
    Bean and Rice Burritos 16
    Italian Beans and Rice 18
    Spaghetti Beans and Rice 20
    Lime Beans and Rice 22
    Black Beans and Rice 24
    Tomato and White Beans 26
    Mediterranean Beans and Rice 28
    Pinto Beans and Rice 30
    Baltimore Beans and Rice 32
    Cajun White Beans and Rice 34
    Granny's Beans and Rice 36
    Beans and Rice Pot Pie 38
    Black Bean and Rice Frittata 40
    Beans and Rice Casserole 42
    Nott-a-Burger 44
    Three Sisters Casserole 46
    Summer Skillet 48

Soups

    Pinto Beans and Rice Soup 52
    Dirty Rice Soup 54
    Taco Soup 56
    Tex-Mex Soup 58
    Peanut Butter Soup 60
    Black Bean Soup 62

White Bean Soup   64
Spaghetti Soup   66
Italian Soup   68
White Bean and Collard Greens Soup   70
Simple Soup   72
Savory Soup   74

Bread, Flour and Pasta

Rice Flour   78
Bean Flour   79
Garbanzo Bean Flatbread   80
Rice Flour Tortillas   81
Rice Flour Bread   82
Rice Flour Pie Crust   83
Chickpea Flour Pie Crust   84
Rice Noodles   85

Desserts

Black Bean Brownies   92
White Bean Blondies   93
Chickpea Cupcakes   94
Chocolate Peanut Butter Dessert Hummus   95
Bean Meringues   96
Rice Pudding   97
Fried Rice Fritter   98
Sweet Tamales   99
Puffed Rice   100
Rice Crepes   101
Cinnamon Beans and Rice   102
Sweet Buns   103
Bean Custard Pie   105

Snacks

Black Bean Crackers   112
Black Bean Dip   113
Hummus   114

    Rice Chips   115
    Garlic Rice Crackers   116
    Rice Cakes   117

Drinks

    Sweet Rice Drink   124
    Chocolate Rice Milk   125
    Rice Wine   126

Miscellaneous

    Instant Rice   130
    Rice Syrup   131
    Rice Syrup Toffee   133
    Hard Candy   134
    Bonus Recipe: Barley Malt Powder   135

Note from the Author   141

Introduction

Two of the main staples in every prepper's pantry are beans and rice. Some of you will look at your buckets full of beans and rice and wonder what to do with them now that you have them. And some of you may already know how to make a few variations of "beans and rice." For these reasons, this book was created to show you how to use these basic ingredients to their full potential. Because they really are the perfect survival food.

There are several reasons why beans and rice are considered to be the ultimate survival food.
- They are inexpensive.
- They are packed full of nutrition and energy.
- If properly stored, they will keep for about 30 years.
- They can be added to just about any recipe to increase the volume.
- They can be used to make a variety of foods other than just "beans and rice."

Can you imagine in a SHTF situation having to eat plain beans and rice every day? Not very good for morale, that's for sure. And most people would hit food fatigue very quickly. Then imagine if you knew many different ways to cook beans and rice so that you had a variety of flavorful meals, snacks, desserts and more? Sounds a lot better right?

Already having the knowledge of how to cook the recipes in this book and to utilize your beans and rice to their full potential will bring you peace of mind in an emergency situation. So the plan is to pick one recipe a week and make it. This will allow you to rotate your stock and teach you how to use it. One of the many rules of prepping is to store what you eat and eat what you store. Otherwise you are just wasting time and money.

The recipes included here contain ingredients other than just beans and rice but they are all things you should be including in your pantry anyway. Going through this book and preparing the recipes will help you understand additional things you may need to prep.

In some of the emergencies you will encounter in your life, you may still have the means to cook normally. But in a situation where you don't have your regular cooking resources (gas, electricity, etc.), you will find that some of these recipes, as written, are not practical. As a prepper, you should be ready for any kind of situation.

This means, that in addition to the dried beans and uncooked rice that you have stored, you should also have canned beans and instant rice. Both of which can be used in the recipes here, allowing you to put a meal together faster and with less resources.

Serving sizes are not listed in the recipes because every one is so different. If the recipe does not yield enough to feed your family for one meal, then you could always double it. This is another reason it is important to go through and make the recipes now so that you know.

As an experienced cook, you know that cook times can vary depending on a lot of things. But for those of you who are a little less experienced, know that there are things that can change how you cook. It is best to try out the recipes now, as mentioned above so that you know what to expect. If you're in a stressful situation and try a new recipe that doesn't turn out right, it can make a bad day even worse.

Hey, comfort meals are a thing for a reason! Also, depending on your herbs/seasonings and your own taste buds, you may need to increase or decrease the amount listed in the recipes.

If you purchased the paperback edition of this book, then there will be a notes section following each recipe. This is where you can write down important information when you try one out. You can record which variation you tried; how well your family liked it; if you need to double the recipe; and anything else that you think is important for the next time you make it. If you purchased the e-book version, the notes section is not included. The app or e-reader that you use should allow you to save comments or notes. However, it would be wise to make sure you have a printed copy of the recipes, along with your notes in case you are not able to use your digital copy.

Finally, it may not seem like there are that many recipes here, but a lot of them have variations which turns one recipe into multiple. Each variation changes the flavor profile so it will taste different. Space comes at a premium when you're a prepper and that translates here as well. I could have repeated all the variations as their own recipe and padded the book out, but I value your space just as much as my own.

NUTRITION

When you combine beans with rice you get a meal that is packed with complete protein, fiber, carbohydrates and a multitude of vitamins and minerals. Beans alone are considered a superfood due to their nutritional value. When you add the benefits of rice to the mix, you get the perfect survival food.

Nutritional values are different for each variety of rice and beans so they are not included here. Just know that when you eat a bowl of beans and rice you are consuming a nutritious, healthy, energy packed bowl of goodness.

Storage

HOW MUCH TO STORE

How much beans and rice should you stockpile? This is a very difficult question to answer but it is a very important one. There are a lot of variables that go into figuring this out as every family's situation, needs and goals are different. It is very important that you take the time to calculate your needs.

Here are a few things to consider when deciding how much you need:
- How long are you preparing for your food storage to last?
- What are the daily calorie needs and total calorie needs for each person?
- Will anyone's daily calorie needs change?
- What percentage of your meals will use beans and rice?

Remember that beans and rice are inexpensive and they last a long time if stored properly. So regardless of how much you have calculated for your needs, always add a little more. Being overprepared is a never a bad thing as needs and goals can change with time.

STORAGE TIPS

The following tips for storing your beans and rice will apply to most of your food storage.

- Make sure your storage location will not have food sitting in direct sunlight.
- The temperature should stay above freezing but below 70° F.
- The storage location should be free from moisture.
- Take precautions to eliminate access for bugs and rodents.
- Rotate your food using the FIFO method. Rotating your food means that you are eating from your stock and replacing it, not just moving it around. This will keep food from just sitting there until it expires. FIFO stands for First In, First Out. With this method new items will be placed in the back so that the oldest items are in the front and will be used first.
- Repackage the food in mylar bags with oxygen absorbers. Then place the mylar bags inside food grade buckets with lids for added protection. Buckets can also be stacked to maximize storage space.
- Write the food name and date you processed it on the mylar bag with a permanent marker.
- Keep a written, up-to-date inventory of everything in your storage. There are many ways to do this so find one that works well for you.
- Know the weight capacity of your shelving and don't overload it. Try to stay away from plastic shelves, as plastic can degrade over time which will reduce its weight capacity.
- If possible, don't store all of your food in one location.
- Ensure you have multiple sources of water to prepare the food in your storage.
- Organize your storage in a way that makes sense to you.
- Inspect your storage regularly for water, bugs, mold and anything else that may cause an issue.

Equivalents

Regardless of whether a recipe calls for fresh or dried ingredients, you can use either. When preparing the recipes in this book, the chart below will help you. It's important to point out that these equivalents are only approximates.

For experienced cooks, you will already know this, but for those who don't, there are a lot of factors that will effect the time it takes to rehydrate vegetables. Since this book is not about that, I chose not to go into it all here. However, you should be familiar with the food that you have stored in your pantry, to include how long it would take to rehydrate. You may be able to just toss them in the pot as your meal cooks or you may need to rehydrate them before hand.

Herbs
1 tablespoon fresh herbs = 1 teaspoon dried flaky herbs = ½ teaspoon dried ground herbs

Beans
A heaping ½ cup of dried beans equals 1 regular size can of beans.

Rice
One cup of uncooked rice equals 2 cups of cooked rice.

Item	Fresh	Dehydrated/Dried
Bell Pepper	1 medium	½ cup
Carrot	2 cups diced	1 cup
Celery	1 stalk	1 heaping tbsp
Cinnamon Stick	1 stick	½ tsp ground
Garlic	1 clove minced	½ tsp
Ginger	1 tbsp minced	½ tsp ground
Lemon	1 medium	2 tsp powder
Lime	1 medium	2 tsp powder
Onion	1 small	1 tbsp
Potato	2 cups diced	1 cup
Tomato, diced	1 ¼ cups	1 cup
Tomato, paste	¾ cup	¼ cup powder
Zucchini	2 ½ cups	1 cup

8 SURVIVING WITH BEANS AND RICE

Main Dishes

Classic Red Beans and Rice

INGREDIENTS
1 ¼ cups dried red kidney beans
1 cup white rice, uncooked
1 tsp dried minced garlic
2 tbsp dried minced onion
1 heaping tbsp dried minced celery
½ cup dried minced green bell pepper
1 tsp salt
½ tsp ground black pepper
1 tbsp Creole or Cajun seasoning
3 cups chicken stock
2 tbsp butter

RECIPE
Start the night before and pour the beans into a pot, covering them with water. The water should be 1 - 2 inches above the beans. Heat over medium-high heat until they start to boil, then turn off the heat. Cover and leave them to soak overnight. When ready to cook, discard the water and fill with fresh water, again 1 - 2 inches above the beans. Simmer the beans for about an hour or until they are tender but firm. The type and age of bean will determine the cooking time.

Once the beans are done, drain the water. Remove ½ cup of beans and mash. In a pot, bring the chicken stock to a boil. Then add all ingredients including the beans, both whole and mashed. Return to a boil. Then reduce heat to low, cover with a lid and cook for about 20 minutes or until the rice is done.

VARIATIONS
You can add meat bones in with the beans while they cook to enhance the flavor of the beans. You can add pork, chicken, turkey or beef to this recipe to create tasty varieties. It's best to cook the meat separately and then add to the pot sometime around the last 20 minutes of cooking.

NOTES

Spanish Beans and Rice

INGREDIENTS
1 ¼ cups dried beans
1 cup white rice, uncooked
1 can fire roasted tomatoes
2 tsp dried minced garlic
3 tbsp dried minced onion
1 cup dried bell pepper
1 tsp chili powder
1 tbsp dried oregano
½ tsp cayenne powder
3 cups vegetable broth
1 tbsp butter

RECIPE
Start the night before and pour the beans into a pot, covering them with water. The water should be 1 - 2 inches above the beans. Heat over medium-high heat until they start to boil, then turn off the heat. Cover and leave them to soak overnight. When ready to cook, discard the water and fill with fresh water, again 1 - 2 inches above the beans. Simmer the beans for about an hour or until they are tender but firm. The type and age of bean will determine the cooking time.

Pour the vegetable broth into a pot and heat to a boil. Add the remaining ingredients except the beans and return to a boil. Reduce the heat to low, cover with a lid and let cook for about 20 minutes. You should leave the lid on during cooking. Once the rice is cooked, remove from the heat, add the beans and serve.

VARIATIONS
You can add meat bones in with the beans while they cook to enhance the flavor of the beans. You can add pork, chicken, turkey or beef to this recipe to create tasty varieties. It's best to cook the meat separately and then add to the pot sometime around the last 20 minutes of cooking.

NOTES

Taco Beans and Rice

INGREDIENTS
1 ¼ cups dried beans
1 cup white rice, uncooked
1 can diced tomatoes
2 cups vegetable broth
1 package of taco seasoning mix OR

Taco Seasoning Mix:
1 tbsp chili powder
1 tsp ground cumin
1 tsp garlic powder
1 tsp ground paprika
½ tsp dried oregano
½ tsp onion powder
¼ tsp salt
¼ tsp ground black pepper
¼ tsp ground red pepper flakes

RECIPE
Start the night before and pour the beans into a pot, covering them with water. The water should be 1 - 2 inches above the beans. Heat over medium-high heat until they start to boil, then turn off the heat. Cover and leave them to soak overnight. When ready to cook, discard the water and fill with fresh water, again 1 - 2 inches above the beans. Simmer the beans for about an hour or until they are tender but firm. The type and age of bean will determine the cooking time.

In a pot, bring the vegetable broth to a boil. Add the rice and return to a boil. Then reduce the heat to low, cover with a lid and cook for about 10 minutes. Add the diced tomatoes and seasonings, then replace the lid. Continue cooking until the rice is done. Once the rice is cooked, remove from heat and add the beans.

VARIATIONS

You can add meat bones in with the beans while they cook to enhance the flavor of the beans. You can add pork, chicken, turkey or beef to this recipe to create tasty varieties. It's best to cook the meat separately and then add to the pot sometime around the last 20 minutes of cooking.

NOTES

_____
_____
_____
_____
_____
_____
_____
_____
_____
_____
_____
_____
_____
_____
_____
_____

Bean and Rice Burritos

INGREDIENTS
1 ¼ cups dried beans
1 cup white rice, uncooked
1 tsp dried minced garlic
2 tbsp dried minced onion
1 heaping tbsp dried minced celery
½ cup dried minced green bell pepper
1 tsp salt
½ tsp ground black pepper
1 tbsp hot sauce
3 cups chicken stock
2 tbsp butter

RECIPE
Start the night before and pour the beans into a pot, covering them with water. The water should be 1 - 2 inches above the beans. Heat over medium-high heat until they start to boil, then turn off the heat. Cover and leave them to soak overnight. When ready to cook, discard the water and fill with fresh water, again 1 - 2 inches above the beans. Simmer the beans for about an hour or until they are tender but firm. The type and age of bean will determine the cooking time.

In a pot bring the chicken stock to a boil. Then add all ingredients except the beans. Return to a boil. Then reduce heat to low, cover with a lid and cook for about 20 minutes. Don't remove the lid during cooking. Once the rice is cooked, remove from heat and add the beans.

Spoon the mixture into a warmed tortilla and wrap. There is a recipe for rice flour tortillas included in this book.

VARIATIONS
You can add meat bones in with the beans while they cook to enhance the flavor of the beans. You can add pork, chicken, turkey or beef to this recipe to create tasty varieties. It's best to cook the meat sepa-

rately and then add to the pot sometime around the last 20 minutes of cooking. Don't forget that you can also add any of your favorites like cheese, sour cream, tomatoes and more.

NOTES

Italian Beans and Rice

INGREDIENTS
1 ¼ cups dried beans
1 cup white rice, uncooked
1 can (14.5 oz) of diced tomatoes
1 can (8 oz) of tomato sauce
¼ tsp dried oregano
¼ tsp dried marjoram
¼ tsp dried basil
¼ tsp dried thyme
¼ tsp dried sage
¼ tsp dried rosemary
3 cups vegetable broth
1 tbsp butter

RECIPE
Start the night before and pour the beans into a pot, covering them with water. The water should be 1 - 2 inches above the beans. Heat over medium-high heat until they start to boil, then turn off the heat. Cover and leave them to soak overnight. When ready to cook, discard the water and fill with fresh water, again 1 - 2 inches above the beans. Simmer the beans for about an hour or until they are tender but firm. The type and age of bean will determine the cooking time.

Add all of the ingredients, including the beans into a pot and cook over medium-high heat. Once it starts to boil, cover, reduce heat and simmer for about 20 minutes or until the rice is fully cooked.

VARIATIONS
You can add meat bones in with the beans while they cook to enhance the flavor of the beans. You can add pork, chicken, turkey or beef to this recipe to create tasty varieties. It's best to cook the meat separately and then add to the pot sometime around the last 20 minutes of cooking.

NOTES

Spaghetti Beans and Rice

INGREDIENTS
1 jar of spaghetti sauce
1 ¼ cups dried beans
1 cup white rice, uncooked
2 cups vegetable broth

RECIPE
Start the night before and pour the beans into a pot, covering them with water. The water should be 1 - 2 inches above the beans. Heat over medium-high heat until they start to boil, then turn off the heat. Cover and leave them to soak overnight. When ready to cook, discard the water and fill with fresh water, again 1 - 2 inches above the beans. Simmer the beans for about an hour or until they are tender but firm. The type and age of bean will determine the cooking time.

Add the rice and vegetable broth to a pot. Heat over medium-high heat until it starts to boil. Cover, reduce heat and simmer for about 20 minutes or until the rice is fully cooked. Add the jar of spaghetti sauce and cooked beans. Heat through and serve.

VARIATIONS
You can add meat bones in with the beans while they cook to enhance the flavor of the beans. You can add pork, chicken, turkey or beef to this recipe to create tasty varieties. It's best to cook the meat separately and then add to the pot sometime around the last 20 minutes of cooking.

NOTES

Lime Beans and Rice

INGREDIENTS
2 cans black beans, drained and rinsed
2 cups white rice, uncooked
2 tbsp oil
1 onion, finely chopped
5 garlic cloves, minced
1 ½ tsp cumin
4 cups chicken stock
3 – 4 tbsp lime juice
4 tbsp finely chopped parsley

RECIPE
Sauté onion in oil until transparent. Then add the garlic and cook for a few minutes more. Stir in the cumin and the uncooked rice. Continue to cook for a few minutes more. Pour in the stock and beans, then bring to boil. Cover, reduce heat and simmer until rice is done. Remove from heat. Add the lime juice and the parsley.

VARIATIONS
Replace the parsley with either coriander or cilantro which will add a unique flavor. You can add pork, chicken, turkey or beef to this recipe to create tasty varieties. It's best to cook the meat separately and then add to the pot sometime around the last 20 minutes of cooking.

NOTES

Black Beans and Rice

INGREDIENTS
1 lb dried black beans
2 cups white rice, uncooked
2 green bell peppers, halved and seeded
8 cups water
1 onion
2 garlic cloves
1 tsp dried oregano
1 tsp ground cumin
1 bay leaf
Salt to taste
1 tbsp vinegar
1 tbsp sugar
¼ cup olive or vegetable oil

RECIPE
Black beans do not need to soak overnight. It will really only save about 30 minutes of cooking and will lose some of the flavor. So for this recipe, it's suggested that you don't soak them.

Add black beans, 8 cups of water and 1 green bell pepper to a stock pot. Bring to a boil. Cover, reduce heat and simmer for and 1 ½ hours or until the beans are almost tender.
Blend the onion, garlic, oregano, cumin, bay leaf and the remaining bell pepper with just a little water until the mixture is smooth. Add the mixture to the beans and bring to a boil again. Once it starts to boil, reduce the heat to simmer. Add the salt, vinegar and sugar, then continue to simmer for about 2 hours or until the mixture becomes thick. Add the vegetable oil to the beans after they have finished cooking.

Cook the rice right before the beans are done. Add the rice, 4 cups of water and a little bit of olive oil. Cover and cook over medium-high heat until it starts to boil. Reduce heat to low and simmer for about 20 minutes or until rice is fully cooked. Then serve the beans and rice together.

VARIATIONS

You can add pork, chicken, turkey or beef to this recipe to create tasty varieties. It's best to cook the meat separately and then add to the pot sometime around the last 20 minutes of cooking.

NOTES

_____
_____
_____
_____
_____
_____
_____
_____
_____
_____
_____
_____
_____
_____
_____
_____

Tomato and White Beans

INGREDIENTS
1 lb dry white beans
1 ½ cups white rice, uncooked
1 head garlic, unpeeled and cut off the top to expose cloves
1 bay leaf
1 large potato, peeled and thinly sliced
1 large tomato, chopped
1 yellow onion, diced
1 bell pepper, seeded and diced
4 tbsp vegetable oil
1 can (15 oz) crushed tomatoes
1 tbsp paprika
1 tsp turmeric
Salt and pepper to taste

RECIPE
Start the night before and pour the beans into a pot, covering them with water. The water should be 1 - 2 inches above the beans. Heat over medium-high heat until they start to boil, then turn off the heat. Cover and leave them to soak overnight. When ready to cook, discard the water and fill with fresh water, again 1 - 2 inches above the beans. Add the head of garlic and bay leaf, then bring to a boil. Cover, reduce heat and simmer until the beans are tender. Cooking times will vary depending on age and type of bean. Once cooked, drain the beans and discard garlic and bay leaf.

Add the potatoes and oil to a pan and fry for a few minutes. Then add the onion and pepper and sauté until the onions are transparent. Add the tomatoes (chopped and crushed), then cook for 2 - 3 minutes.

Add everything, including the rice to a large pot with 3 cups of water and bring to a boil. Cover, reduce heat and simmer until the rice is cooked which should be about 20 minutes. It should have a soupy consistency and you may need to add a little water during cooking to maintain that consistency.

VARIATIONS

You can add meat bones in with the beans while they cook to enhance the flavor of the beans. You can add pork, chicken, turkey or beef to this recipe to create tasty varieties. It's best to cook the meat separately and then add to the pot sometime around the last 20 minutes of cooking.

NOTES

Mediterranean Beans and Rice

INGREDIENTS
1 lb Great Northern White beans
2 cups white rice, uncooked
2 stalks celery, chopped
1 small can black olives
Juice of 1 lemon
½ cup fresh chopped parsley
2 tsp dried dill weed

RECIPE
Start the night before and pour the beans into a pot, covering them with water. The water should be 1 - 2 inches above the beans. Heat over medium-high heat until they start to boil, then turn off the heat. Cover and leave them to soak overnight. When ready to cook, discard the water and fill with fresh water, again 1 - 2 inches above the beans. Simmer the beans for about an hour or until they are tender but firm. The type and age of bean will determine the cooking time.

Add the rice, 4 cups of water and a little bit of olive oil to a pot. Cover and cook over medium-high heat until it starts to boil. Reduce heat to low and simmer for about 20 minutes or until rice is fully cooked.

While the rice is cooking add the beans, onion, celery and olives to a pan. Fry for a few minutes to soften. Then stir in the lemon juice and parsley, cooking for a few more minutes to heat through. Add salt and pepper to taste. Add the dill weed to the rice, then serve together with the beans.

VARIATIONS
You can add meat bones in with the beans while they cook to enhance the flavor of the beans. You can add pork, chicken, turkey or beef to this recipe to create tasty varieties. It's best to cook the meat separately and then add to the pot sometime around the last 20 minutes of cooking.

NOTES

Pinto Beans and Rice

INGREDIENTS
1 lb pinto beans
2 cups white rice, uncooked
2 tsp ground cumin
1 tsp chili powder
1 can diced tomatoes with green chilies, drained
Juice of 1 small lime
¼ cup fresh cilantro, chopped
Salt and pepper to taste

RECIPE
Start the night before and pour the beans into a pot, covering them with water. The water should be 1 - 2 inches above the beans. Heat over medium-high heat until they start to boil, then turn off the heat. Cover and leave them to soak overnight. When ready to cook, discard the water and fill with fresh water, again 1 - 2 inches above the beans. Simmer the beans for about an hour or until they are tender but firm. The type and age of bean will determine the cooking time.

Once the beans are cooked, drain the water and return the beans to the pot. Add the cumin, chili powder, and onion. Fry for a few minutes, then add the tomatoes, lime juice and salt and pepper to taste. Cook until the tomatoes are soft.

Meanwhile, add the rice, 4 cups of water and a little bit of olive oil to a pot. Cover and cook over medium-high heat until it starts to boil. Reduce heat to low and simmer for about 20 minutes or until rice is fully cooked. Stir the cilantro into the rice and serve together with the beans.

VARIATIONS
You can add meat bones in with the beans while they cook to enhance the flavor of the beans. You can add pork, chicken, turkey or beef to

this recipe to create tasty varieties. It's best to cook the meat separately and then add to the pot sometime around the last 20 minutes of cooking.

NOTES

Baltimore Beans and Rice

INGREDIENTS
1 lb black eyed peas
2 cups white rice, uncooked
2 cups chopped kale or spinach
2 tsp apple cider vinegar
2 tsp Worcestershire sauce
½ cup corn
1 tsp Old Bay or any Chesapeake-style seafood seasoning
Salt and pepper to taste

RECIPE
Start the night before and pour the beans into a pot, covering them with water. The water should be 1 - 2 inches above the beans. Heat over medium-high heat until they start to boil, then turn off the heat. Cover and leave them to soak overnight. When ready to cook, discard the water and fill with fresh water, again 1 - 2 inches above the beans. Simmer the beans for about an hour or until they are tender but firm. The type and age of bean will determine the cooking time.

Drain and rinse the beans. Return the beans to the pot and add the kale or spinach and the onion. Sauté until the leafy greens are wilted. Add the vinegar, Worcestershire sauce and corn, then heat through. Add salt and pepper to taste.

Meanwhile, add the rice, 4 cups of water and a little bit of olive oil to a pot. Cover and cook over medium-high heat until it starts to boil. Reduce heat to low and simmer for about 20 minutes or until rice is fully cooked. Sprinkle the Old Bay seasoning on the rice and serve with the beans.

VARIATIONS
You can add meat bones in with the beans while they cook to enhance the flavor of the beans. You can add pork, chicken, turkey or beef to

this recipe to create tasty varieties. It's best to cook the meat separately and then add to the pot sometime around the last 20 minutes of cooking.

NOTES

Cajun White Beans and Rice

INGREDIENTS
1 lb uncooked white beans
2 cups white rice, uncooked
2 tbsp vegetable oil
1 yellow onion, diced
2 celery stalks, diced
1 green bell pepper, diced
6 garlic cloves, minced
½ cup vegetable broth
2 bay leaves
1 tsp ground paprika
½ tsp dried thyme
¼ tsp ground cayenne pepper
Salt and pepper to taste

RECIPE
Start the night before and pour the beans into a pot, covering them with water. The water should be 1 - 2 inches above the beans. Heat over medium-high heat until they start to boil, then turn off the heat. Cover and leave them to soak overnight. When ready to cook, discard the water and fill with fresh water, again 1 - 2 inches above the beans. Simmer the beans for about an hour or until they are tender but firm. The type and age of bean will determine the cooking time.

Add oil and onion in a pot and sauté until the onion is transparent. Add the celery, garlic and pepper and cook until tender. Add beans and the remaining ingredients (except the rice). Bring to a boil, cover, reduce heat and simmer for 15 minutes.

Meanwhile, add the rice, 4 cups of water and a little bit of olive oil to a pot. Cover and cook over medium-high heat until it starts to boil. Reduce heat to low and simmer for about 20 minutes or until rice is fully cooked. Serve the beans over rice.

VARIATIONS

You can add meat bones in with the beans while they cook to enhance the flavor of the beans. You can add pork, chicken, turkey or beef to this recipe to create tasty varieties. It's best to cook the meat separately and then add to the pot sometime around the last 20 minutes of cooking.

NOTES

Granny's Beans and Rice

INGREDIENTS
2 cups white rice, uncooked
1 ½ cups mixed dried beans (use your favorites)
1 onion, thinly sliced
28 oz diced tomatoes
2 tbsp oil
Salt, pepper, onion powder and garlic powder to taste

RECIPE
Start the night before and pour the beans into a pot, covering them with water. The water should be 1 - 2 inches above the beans. Heat over medium-high heat until they start to boil, then turn off the heat. Cover and leave them to soak overnight. When ready to cook, discard the water and fill with fresh water, again 1 - 2 inches above the beans. Simmer the beans for about an hour or until they are tender but firm. The type and age of bean will determine the cooking time.

Heat oil in a pan and sauté onions until soft and translucent. Add tomatoes and beans to the pan, then seasonings to taste. Cook for about 20 minutes.

Meanwhile, add the rice, 4 cups of water and a little bit of olive oil to a pot. Cover and cook over medium-high heat until it starts to boil. Reduce heat to low and simmer for about 20 minutes or until rice is fully cooked. Once both are done, serve together.

VARIATIONS
You can add meat bones in with the beans while they cook to enhance the flavor of the beans. You can add pork, chicken, turkey or beef to this recipe to create tasty varieties. It's best to cook the meat separately and then add to the pot sometime around the last 20 minutes of cooking.

NOTES

Beans and Rice Pot Pie

INGREDIENTS
1 ½ cups water
¾ cup white rice, uncooked
2 celery stalks, chopped
1 bell pepper, chopped
1 medium onion, chopped
1 can black beans, drained
1 can (14.5 oz) diced tomatoes
1 can (6 oz) tomato paste
1 ¼ tbsp Cajun seasonings
¼ tsp salt
Pie crust top and bottom (see recipe for rice or bean flour pie crust)

RECIPE
Preheat oven to 425° F.

Heat water and rice in a pot until boiling. Reduce heat, cover and simmer for about 10 minutes. Add celery, bell pepper and onion. Turn up the heat and let boil for 1 minute, then reduce the heat. Cook until rice is tender and most of the water is gone. Remove from heat.

Roll out pie dough into pie plate.

Mix beans, tomatoes, tomato paste and 1 tablespoon of Cajun seasoning together and then add the rice mixture. Spoon into pie plate. Top with second pie crust and seal the edges.

Brush the pie crust top lightly with water. Mix salt and ¼ teaspoon of Cajun seasoning, then sprinkle evenly across the top of the pie. Cut a few slits into the top crust for steam to escape.

Bake about 30 minutes or until the crust is nice and golden brown. Depending on how your oven cooks, you may need to cover the edges of the pie crust with aluminum foil to prevent burning.

VARIATIONS

You can add pork, chicken, turkey or beef to this recipe to create tasty varieties. It's best to cook the meat separately and then add to the filling mix before baking. Also, you could use a lot of the different Main Dish recipes as the filler instead. Now you have about a hundred variations!

NOTES

Black Bean and Rice Frittata

INGREDIENTS
1 can black beans, drained
1 cup cooked rice
1 onion, diced
1 bell pepper, diced
1 jalapeno, seeded and diced
2 garlic cloves, minced
Salt and pepper to taste
1 tsp ground cumin
½ tsp cayenne pepper
½ tsp fresh oregano
6 eggs
½ cup milk
2 tbsp bacon grease

RECIPE
Preheat the oven to 375° F.

Add the bacon grease, onion, bell pepper and jalapeno to an oven safe skillet and sauté until soft. Add the garlic, salt, pepper, cumin, cayenne and oregano, then cook for an additional 2 minutes. Stir in the beans and rice.

Whisk together the eggs, milk and a pinch of salt and pepper. (And a few dashes of hot sauce if you want to turn up the heat) Pour the mixture into the skillet with the beans and rice. Then mix well.

Place the skillet in the oven and bake for about 20 minutes or until no longer jiggly.

VARIATIONS
You can add pork, chicken, turkey or beef to this recipe to create tasty varieties. It's best to cook the meat separately and then add to the

skillet right before putting it into the oven. If you have the ingredients on hand to make a fresh salsa then this will taste great with some salsa on top.

NOTES

Beans and Rice Casserole

INGREDIENTS
1 can black beans, rinsed and drained
1 can (14.5 oz) diced tomatoes
1 can (8 oz) tomato sauce
1 jar salsa 8 oz
2 cups cooked rice
1 cup sour cream
2 cups shredded cheddar cheese

RECIPE
Preheat the oven to 350° F.

Combine all the ingredients and pour into a greased 9" x 13" pan. Bake uncovered for about 30 minutes or until the cheese is melted.

VARIATIONS
You can add pork, chicken, turkey or beef to this recipe to create tasty varieties. It's best to cook the meat separately and then add to the pan right before putting it into the oven.

NOTES

Nott-a-Burger

INGREDIENTS
½ cup white rice, uncooked
½ cup onion, diced
1 can black beans rinsed and drained
2 garlic cloves, minced
2 tsp steak seasoning
½ tsp Creole or Cajun seasoning
½ tsp black pepper
1 tsp Worcestershire sauce (alternatives: steak sauce or bbq sauce)
2 ½ cups water
1 egg
½ cup bread crumbs

RECIPE
Preheat oven to 375° F.

Add the rice, 1 ½ cups of water and a little bit of olive oil to a pot. Cover and cook over medium-high heat until it starts to boil. Reduce heat to low and simmer for about 20 minutes or until rice is soft. You want this rice to be softer than normal so that it will mash easier.

Sauté onion in oil (or bacon grease) until soft. Add the beans, garlic, seasonings, sauce and 1 cup water to the pan. Simmer for about 10 minutes or until the liquid has evaporated.

Transfer the mixture to a food processor and blend until smooth. Or you can transfer to a bowl and use a potato masher. Let the mixture cool. Add the egg and bread crumbs, then mix again until smooth.

Form the mixture into patties and place on a baking sheet. Bake for about 20 minutes, then flip. Bake an additional 10 minutes or until crisp.

These patties can be served on a bun like hamburgers or can be smothered with gravy (or ketchup, or steak sauce, etc.).

VARIATIONS
You can add little bits of bacon or cooked ground meat to the mix.

NOTES

Three Sisters Casserole

INGREDIENTS
1 ¼ cups yellow cornmeal
½ cup all-purpose flour
2 tsp baking powder
1 ½ tsp salt
2 tbsp unsalted butter, melted
½ cup milk
½ cup water
3 tbsp bacon grease
1 onion, diced
4 garlic cloves, minced
1 lb butternut squash
1 can fire roasted tomatoes
2 tbsp tomato paste
1 tsp ground coriander
1 ½ tsp ground cumin
½ tsp chili powder
¼ tsp smoke paprika
¾ cup vegetable broth
1 cup corn
1 can kidney beans
1 cup white rice, uncooked

RECIPE
Preheat oven to 350° F and grease a 9"x 13" baking dish.

Add the rice, 2 cups of water and a little bit of olive oil to a pot. Cover and cook over medium-high heat until it starts to boil. Reduce heat to low and simmer for about 20 minutes or until rice is fully cooked.

Meanwhile, in a dutch oven, over medium heat add the oil and onions. Sauté until soft and translucent. Add the garlic and cook for an additional 1 – 2 minutes. Add in the squash, tomatoes, tomato paste, spices and ½ teaspoon salt. Stir and bring to a boil. Cover, reduce heat and simmer for about 20 minutes or until the squash is tender.

While that simmers, mix the cornmeal, flour, baking powder and 1 teaspoon salt in a bowl. Slowly stir in the butter, milk and water just until combined. Set aside for about 10 minutes.

Once the squash is tender, stir in the rice, beans and corn and cook for about 5 minutes or until the mixture has thickened slightly. Then pour into the baking dish.

Top the casserole with generous biscuit sized clumps of the cornbread mix, it doesn't have to be even and should not cover the top completely. Bake for about 20 minutes or until the cornbread is golden brown.

VARIATIONS

You can add pork, chicken, turkey or beef to this recipe to create tasty varieties. It's best to cook the meat separately and then add to the pan right before putting into the oven.

NOTES

_____
_____
_____
_____
_____
_____
_____
_____
_____
_____

Summer Skillet

INGREDIENTS
2 cups summer squash, diced
1 onion, diced
2 cups corn
2 cups cooked beans
2 cups cooked rice
4 tbsp bacon grease (or vegetable oil but I don't recommend)
2 tbsp fresh basil
Salt and pepper to taste

RECIPE
Heat the bacon grease in a large skillet with high heat. Add the onion and squash. Then sauté until soft and the onions start turning golden. Add the corn and reduce the heat to medium. Cook for an additional 5 minutes.

Add the beans and rice, then heat through. Sprinkle with salt, pepper and basil before serving.

VARIATIONS
You can add pork, chicken, turkey or beef to this recipe to create tasty varieties. It's best to cook the meat separately and then add to the pot at the end to heat through.

NOTES

SOUPS

Soups

Pinto Beans and Rice Soup

INGREDIENTS
1 ⅔ cups dried pinto beans
¾ cup white rice, uncooked
2 tbsp olive oil
1 onion, diced
1 bell pepper, diced
1 potato, diced
1 garlic clove, minced
5 tomatoes, diced
Salt to taste
6 cups water

RECIPE
Soak the pinto beans in cold water overnight. Rinse and drain.
Add olive oil, onion, garlic and bell pepper in pot and sauté over medium heat for about 5 minutes. Add a pinch of salt and the potatoes and sauté for about another 8 minutes. Reduce the heat to medium-low, then add the tomatoes and the pinto beans. Pour in 6 cups cold water, cover and cook until the beans are almost done which should be about an hour. Add in the rice and cook for an additional 20 – 30 minutes or until the rice is done.

VARIATIONS
Add your choice of meat to turn this one recipe into multiple variations. It's best to cook the meat separately and add to the soup just before it's done so that the meat is heated through.

NOTES

Dirty Rice Soup

INGREDIENTS
2 cans red beans, rinsed and drained
1 cup white rice, uncooked
1 onion, diced
5 garlic cloves, minced
2 carrots, diced
1 bell pepper, diced
1 stalk celery, diced
8 cups vegetable broth
28 oz can diced tomatoes
1 cup corn
1 tsp pepper
½ tsp salt
½ tsp cayenne pepper
½ tsp dried thyme
½ tsp dried oregano
1 tbsp chili powder
1 tbsp smoke paprika
1 tbsp ground cumin
2 tbsp olive oil

RECIPE
Heat oil in pan over medium heat. Add the onions, garlic and carrots. Sauté until the onions are soft but not browned. Add the bell pepper, celery, vegetable broth, tomatoes, corn, beans and all the spices.
Bring to a slow boil and then add the rice. Cover, reduce heat and simmer for about 20 -30 minutes, stirring occasionally until the rice is fully cooked.

VARIATIONS
Add your choice of meat to turn this one recipe into multiple variations. It's best to cook the meat separately and add to the soup just before it's done so that the meat is heated through.

NOTES

Taco Soup

INGREDIENTS
2 cans black beans, rinsed and drained
½ cup white rice, uncooked
4 - 5 cups vegetable broth
2 tbsp taco seasoning mix
1 cup tomato sauce

RECIPE
This is a simple one, just add all the ingredients into a pot on the stove. Cook over medium-high heat until it starts to boil. Cover, reduce heat and simmer for about 20 minutes or until the rice is fully cooked.

VARIATIONS
Add your choice of meat to turn this one recipe into multiple variations. It's best to cook the meat separately and add to the soup just before it's done so that the meat is heated through.

NOTES

Tex-Mex Soup

INGREDIENTS
1 can black beans, rinsed and drained
1 can pinto beans, rinsed and drained
1 tbsp olive oil
1 onion diced
2 garlic cloves minced
1 tsp ground cumin
Salt and pepper to taste
1 can (15 oz) diced tomatoes with green chilies
1 cup white rice, uncooked
¼ cup fresh cilantro, chopped

RECIPE
Add the rice, 2 cups of water and a little bit of olive oil to a pot. Cover and cook over medium-high heat until it starts to boil. Reduce heat to low and simmer for about 20 minutes or until rice is fully cooked. Meanwhile, heat the oil in a separate pot over medium heat. Add the onion and sauté until soft. Add the garlic, cumin, salt and pepper and cook for a few minutes more. Then add the tomatoes, beans and 6 cups water. Bring to a boil, then reduce heat to simmer. Simmer for about 15 minutes.
Remove ½ cup of beans with no liquid and mash with a fork. Then return the mixture back to the pot along with the rice and cilantro. Cook for an additional 5 – 10 minutes or until heated through and the soup slightly thickens. Season with additional salt and pepper to taste.

VARIATIONS
Add your choice of meat to turn this one recipe into multiple variations. It's best to cook the meat separately and add to the soup just before it's done so that the meat is heated through.

NOTES

Peanut Butter Soup

INGREDIENTS
1 can black eyed peas
1 cup white rice, uncooked
4 cups vegetable broth
4 cups water
1 onion, diced
2 tbsp fresh ginger, minced
1 tsp salt
1 bunch collard greens, chopped
¾ cup peanut butter, unsalted
½ cup tomato paste
Hot sauce to taste
Optional: chopped peanuts to garnish

RECIPE
Add the vegetable broth and 2 cups water to a stock pot and bring to a boil. Add the onion, ginger, garlic and salt. Then cook on medium-low heat for about 20 minutes.

Meanwhile, add the rice, 2 cups of water and a little bit of olive oil to a pot. Cover and cook over medium-high heat until it starts to boil. Reduce heat to low and simmer for about 20 minutes or until rice is fully cooked.
Mix the peanut butter and tomato paste in a bowl. Transfer 1 to 2 cups of the hot broth to the bowl. Stir the mixture until smooth and then add back to the stock pot. Stir in the collard greens and black eyed peas. Add some hot sauce to taste. Simmer for about another 15 minutes.

Serve over rice and sprinkle with peanuts.

VARIATIONS
I've never attempted to add anything to this recipe because of the

unique flavor profile but you could try if you like. The most likely choice would be bacon or ham.

NOTES

Black Bean Soup

INGREDIENTS
3 can black beans, drained but not rinsed
1 cup white rice, uncooked
1 onion, diced
2 garlic cloves, minced
1 tsp chili powder
2 tsp ground cumin
2 tsp dried oregano
3 cups vegetable broth
½ tsp salt
1 bay leaf
2 tbsp cornstarch, mixed with 2 tbsp cold water
2 tbsp cooking oil
2 cups water

RECIPE
Mash 1 can of beans and set aside. Then heat oil in pot over medium-high heat, add onions and sauté until soft. Add garlic, chili powder, cumin, oregano and cook until garlic is soft which should be about 5 minutes.
Meanwhile, add the rice, 2 cups of water and a little bit of olive oil to a pot. Cover and cook over medium-high heat until it starts to boil. Reduce heat to low and simmer for about 20 minutes or until rice is fully cooked.
Add vegetable broth, salt, bay leaf and beans (both canned and mashed) to the first pot, then bring to a boil. Reduce heat to medium-low and add the cornstarch mixture. Cover and simmer for about 15 minutes. When done, remove the bay leaf and serve over rice.

VARIATIONS
Add your choice of meat to turn this one recipe into multiple variations. It's best to cook the meat separately and add to the soup just before it's done so that the meat is heated through.

NOTES

White Bean Soup

INGREDIENTS
1 can white beans
¾ cup white rice, uncooked
1 tbsp olive oil
3 garlic cloves, minced
4 cups vegetable broth
1 tsp dried basil
1 tsp dried thyme
1 tsp dried oregano
2 cups broccoli florets, chopped
2 cups fresh spinach, chopped

RECIPE
Heat oil over medium heat and sauté garlic for 1 minute. Add rice and cook an additional 2 minutes. Stir in the broth, broccoli and herbs, then bring to a boil. Reduce heat, cover and simmer for about 10 minutes. Add the beans and spinach, then continue to cook until the rice is done.

VARIATIONS
Add your choice of meat to turn this one recipe into multiple variations. It's best to cook the meat separately and add to the soup just before it's done so that the meat is heated through.

NOTES

Spaghetti Soup

INGREDIENTS
1 jar of spaghetti sauce
1 can of kidney beans, rinsed and drained
1 cup white rice, uncooked
1 cup zucchini, shredded
2 cups water
2 cups vegetable broth

RECIPE
Another easy one here, just toss all the ingredients into a pot, cover and simmer over medium heat until the rice is done.

NOTE
You can use a cheese shredder (with big holes) to make long thick shreds of the zucchini if you slice it at an angle.

VARIATIONS
Add your choice of meat to turn this one recipe into multiple variations. It's best to cook the meat separately and add to the soup just before it's done so that the meat is heated through.

NOTES

Italian Soup

INGREDIENTS
½ cup white rice, uncooked
2 cans white beans, rinsed and drained
6 cups vegetable broth
1 cup water
1 cup tomato sauce
1 onion, diced
4 garlic cloves, minced
2 tomatoes, diced
1 heaping tbsp of Italian seasonings
Salt and pepper to taste
¼ tsp chili powder
½ cup fresh basil, chopped

RECIPE
Prepare the rice first by adding the rice, 1 cup of water and a little bit of olive oil to a pot. Cover and cook over medium-high heat until it starts to boil. Reduce heat to low and simmer for about 20 minutes or until rice is fully cooked.

Meanwhile, add the onion, garlic and ½ cup of broth to a large pot. Sauté for about 8 minutes or until tender. Add the remaining broth, tomato sauce, Italian seasonings, salt, pepper and chili powder, then bring to a boil. Immediately turn down to medium heat, cover and cook for about 10 minutes. Add the tomatoes and cook for another 10 minutes.

Add the beans, rice and basil to the pot. Bring to a low boil, then simmer for another 10 minutes.

VARIATIONS
Add your choice of meat to turn this one recipe into multiple variations. It's best to cook the meat separately and add to the soup just before it's done so that the meat is heated through.

NOTES

White Bean and Collard Greens Soup

INGREDIENTS
2 cups dried navy beans
2 cups white rice, uncooked
1 tbsp olive oil
2 onions, diced
4 carrots, diced
3 stalks celery, diced
Salt and pepper to taste
2 Bay leaves
2 tsp dried thyme
4 cups vegetable broth
4 cups water
3 cups tomatoes, strained
2 bunches collard greens, chopped
1 pinch of crushed red pepper flakes (optionally use hot sauce)

RECIPE
Start the night before and pour the beans into a pot, covering them with water. The water should be 1 - 2 inches above the beans. Heat over medium-high heat until they start to boil, then turn off the heat. Cover and leave them to soak overnight. When ready to cook, discard the water.

Add olive oil, onions, carrots and celery in a pot. Sauté over medium heat for about 8 minutes or until soft. Add salt, pepper, bay leaves, thyme, broth, 3 cups water, rice and beans. Bring to a boil, cover, reduce heat and simmer for about an hour. Just until beans start to become tender.
Add tomatoes and collard greens to pot, then replace the lid. Simmer until beans, rice and collards are tender which should be about 20 minutes. Add water as needed to keep soup consistency.

Sprinkle with red pepper flakes or use a dash of hot sauce when served.

VARIATIONS

Add your choice of meat or meat bones to turn this one recipe into multiple variations.

NOTES

Simple Soup

INGREDIENTS
1 cup white rice, uncooked
1 can beans, drained
1 – 2 chicken or beef bouillon cubes
3 - 4 cups water

RECIPE
Combine all the ingredients into a pot, cover and simmer for about 15 – 20 minutes or until the rice is done. Adjust water amount to desired consistency. You can also mash some of the beans when you first start cooking to thicken the soup.

VARIATIONS
There are a lot of choices for variations with this soup. You could add your choice of meat or vegetables. You could add cream or half and half when serving. If adding this, make sure you add it into the bowl you are serving in and do not cook it in the soup. Also, instead of bouillon cubes you could use dry soup packets like mushroom, french onion, or others. My favorite variation is using mushroom soup mix and cream!

NOTES

Savory Soup

INGREDIENTS
2 whole onions
1 cup white rice, uncooked
2 – 3 cups cooked black beans
4 – 5 cups vegetable broth
4 garlic cloves, minced
1 tsp cumin
2 tsp chili powder
1 tbsp vegetable oil

RECIPE
Leave the peels on the onions and bake at 400° F for about an hour. The outer layer of skin will probably blacken but that is okay. Remove the onions from the oven and peel away the blackened portions. The blackened peel can be discarded.

Sauté the garlic and oil in a soup pot for about 4 – 5 minutes. Add the onion, 2 cups of vegetable broth and spices, then simmer over low heat for a few minutes. Add 1 cup of beans and 2 cups of vegetable broth and bring back to a simmer. Use a potato masher to mash up the mix in the soup pot. Alternatively, you could pour the mix into a blender. Either way, mash until smooth.

Now add the remaining ingredients, return to a low simmer, cover and cook until the rice is done.

Note: If you decide to use a blender, be careful with the hot liquid. The heat could build up while you're blending and pop the lid off!

VARIATIONS
Add your choice of meat to turn this one recipe into multiple variations. It's best to cook the meat separately and add to the soup when adding the rice.

NOTES

Bread, Flour and Pasta

Rice Flour

1 cup of uncooked rice yields about 1 ½ cups of rice flour.

INGREDIENTS
White rice, uncooked

RECIPE
Add the uncooked rice to the grain mill and grind until you get a fine consistency. You most likely will need to run the rice through the mill more than once. Make sure to read the instructions for your particular grain mill first so you know how much you can grind at a time.

Continue to run the rice through the grain mill until the flour has reached a very fine consistency. The flour will not combine well with other ingredients if it is too thick.

Store the rice flour in an airtight container. It will last much longer if kept in the freezer. But since it's so easy to grind the flour, there's no need to grind up a large amount of rice at once. Just grind in small batches as needed. If the rice flour ever has a waxy crayon smell then it has gone rancid.

Don't use a blender or food processor to make rice flour. There are many options for grain mills both electric and manual. As a prepper, you should have a manual powered grain mill in your preps.

USING RICE FLOUR
Why use rice flour? Well, grinding your own rice flour at home is a lot less expensive than using store bought wheat flour. And you can use it in all of your favorite recipes. Although, it's important to note that it's not always a 1:1 substitute for wheat flour. There are already many recipes out there with rice flour that have been tried and tested, or you can just experiment on your own. It's also good as a thickening agent in soups and can be used to coat fried vegetables which will make them even tastier.

Bean Flour

Flour yields vary by bean.

INGREDIENTS
Beans, dried

RECIPE
Making bean flour is really simple, you just grind up the beans in a grain mill to a fine flour texture. You can roast the beans for about 20 minutes at 400° F to give the flour a nuttier flavor and to make grinding less work.

USING BEAN FLOUR
You can substitute bean flour for wheat flour in most recipes. But there are a few important things to understand. First, it will produce variations in color, texture and flavor depending on the type of bean used. Second, bean flours do not contain gluten which gives baked goods their elasticity. And lastly, some bean flours have a smell when cooked. Some people like the smell while others do not.

Bean flour may not seem like the best choice based on the above notes, however, in a long term SHTF situation, it may become a necessity. Beans are easier to grow and harvest compared to wheat. So learn how to use it now to make recipes your family will love. Once you understand the ins and out of cooking with bean flour then the differences from wheat flour are not an issue.

In addition to using bean flour to make baked goods, it can be used in a variety of things like gravies, sauces, soup thickeners and dips for snacking. To make a bean dip, you just add enough water to the flour to create the consistency you want and then add seasonings. Let your creativity and taste buds go wild to create something your family will love.

Garbanzo Bean Flatbread

INGREDIENTS
1 cup garbanzo bean flour
½ onion, thinly sliced
1 ¾ cups water
¾ tsp salt
1 tsp ground black pepper
5 tbsp extra virgin olive oil
Fresh rosemary leaves (or dried if you prefer)

RECIPE
Sift the flour into a bowl, then add the salt and pepper. Next, slowly whisk in the water. Make sure there are no clumps. Stir in 2 tablespoons of the olive oil. Cover and let sit for at least an hour. However, it can be left for up to 12 hours. As it sits, the batter will thicken to the consistency of heavy cream.

Preheat oven to 400° F.

Place a 10 inch cast iron skillet over medium heat. Add the onion and 2 – 3 tablespoons of oil into the pan, then sauté for about one minute. Pour in the batter and rosemary and drizzle some olive oil on top. Place the pan in the oven and bake for about 20 – 30 minutes or until firm. Then broil until the top is golden brown.

Can be served warm or cool.

Rice Flour Tortillas

INGREDIENTS
1 cup rice flour
¼ tsp salt
1 cup water
Oil to grease hands

RECIPE

Add the water to a pot and heat to boil. Stir flour and salt in a bowl. Add ¾ cup of boiling water to the rice slowly and stir. You need to have a crumbly consistency and can add more water if needed. Cover the bowl and let it rest for about 10 minutes.

Grease your hands with the oil and then knead the crumbly consistency into a dough. Shape it into a log and then cut into 6 golf ball size pieces. Then roll each piece into a tortilla. If you want to stack the uncooked pieces remember to place parchment paper between each one so they do not stick together.

Heat a large nonstick pan over medium-high heat. Cook for about 30 seconds to 2 minutes on each side, then remove. Repeat for the remaining tortillas. Remember to cover the cooked tortillas so they stay warm.

Rice Flour Bread

INGREDIENTS
2 cups rice flour
1 tsp salt
1 tsp instant dry yeast
1 ½ tsp sugar
½ cup corn flour
1 tbsp oil
Warm water

RECIPE
Combine yeast, sugar and 2 tablespoons of warm water. Mix well and cover, then let it sit for about 10 minutes.

Combine the rice flour, corn flour, yeast-sugar mixture, oil and salt. Then mix well using enough warm water to form a thick dough consistency. Place the batter in a greased rectangular 7"x 3" pan and cover with a warm damp cloth. Let it rise for about 45 minutes.

Preheat oven to 400° F and then bake for about 40 minutes.

Rice Flour Pie Crust

INGREDIENTS
1 cup rice flour
1 tbsp sugar
½ tsp salt
¼ tsp baking powder
⅓ cup vegetable shortening
3 tbsp cold water
½ tsp vanilla extract

NOTE
If making for a savory dish like a pot pie, you can omit the vanilla. Also, this only makes 1 pie crust so double the recipe if you need a top crust.

RECIPE
Combine the rice flour, sugar, salt and baking powder in a bowl, then mix well. Cut in the shortening until the mixture looks like sand. Add the water and vanilla extract, then form into a dough.

This crust will be crumblier than a regular flour pie dough. To make it easier to roll out, you should place the dough into the freezer for a while. Then roll out onto parchment paper and stick in the freezer once again before placing it in the pie pan.

Bake as directed in the recipe you are using.

Chickpea Flour Pie Crust

INGREDIENTS
1 ½ cups chickpea flour
½ tsp salt
½ tbsp sugar
1 stick butter, cubed and very cold
1 cup water with ice cubes

NOTE
Makes 1 crust, double if you need a top and bottom. Also, this crust only pairs well with savory dishes due to its flavor. Maybe you will like it with sweet recipes as well though.

RECIPE
Combine chickpea flour, salt and sugar in a bowl, then mix well. Cut cold butter cubes into mixture until a crumbly dough forms.

Add the iced water (minus the ice cubes) 1 tablespoon at a time. You need to mix the dough after adding each tablespoon of water and continue adding more water until the dough comes together in a nice ball.

Place the tightly covered dough in the freezer for 2 hours. Remove from the freezer and roll out on a floured surface.

Place into pie pan and bake according to your recipe.

Rice Noodles

INGREDIENTS
1 ¼ cups rice flour
2 tbsp cornstarch
½ tsp salt
1 ¼ cups water
1 tsp vegetable oil

RECIPE
For this recipe you will need a flat pan (like a pie tin) that fits inside a steamer pot.

Mix the rice flour, cornstarch, salt and water together. Add 1 teaspoon of oil to the mixture. Pour the mixture through a fine-mesh strainer, then cover and let sit for about 30 minutes.

Turn on the heat and get your steamer ready.

Once the steamer is ready, pour the rice mixture into the flat bottom pan. Make sure you rotate the pan around until the bottom is covered evenly with a thin layer. Place the pan inside the steamer and cook for about 5 – 8 minutes. The exact time will depend on the size of the pan and the thickness of the mixture.

Once the mixture is cooked, carefully transfer the noodle sheet from the pan to an oiled cutting board. Use a rolling cutter to slice into noodles.

NOTES

NOTES

NOTES

NOTES

DESSERTS

Desserts

NOTE

Don't tell your taste testers that these desserts are different. Just make and let them enjoy. If you want to tell them after they have raved on about how good these desserts are, well that's on you. But seriously, what kid (or adult) would want to touch a brownie made from beans.

Black Bean Brownies

INGREDIENTS
1 ½ cups cooked black beans
2 tbsp cocoa powder
½ cup quick oats
¼ tsp salt
⅓ cup maple syrup or honey
2 tbsp sugar
¼ cup vegetable oil (or coconut oil)
2 tsp pure vanilla extract
½ tsp baking powder
⅔ cup chocolate chips

RECIPE
Preheat oven to 350° F and grease an 8" x 8" pan.

Combine all ingredients, except for the chocolate chips, in a food processor and blend until completely smooth. This can also be done manually in a situation with no electricity but will take some time. After blended, add in the chocolate chips and pour into the pan. Cook for about 15 – 18 minutes.
Let cool for at least 10 minutes.

NOTE
If they seem a little undercooked, place them in a cool place, preferably a fridge, for a while and they will firm up.

VARIATIONS
You can add walnuts or another preferred nut. Either sprinkle on top or bake right in.

White Bean Blondies

INGREDIENTS
1 ½ cups cooked white beans
1 tsp baking powder
¼ tsp salt
¼ tsp baking soda
¾ cup sugar
⅓ cup flour
¼ cup applesauce
3 tbsp oil
½ cup chocolate chips

RECIPE
Preheat oven to 350° F and grease an 8" x 8" pan.

Drain and rinse the beans very well. Blend all ingredients, except the chocolate chips, in a food processor until very smooth. This can also be done manually in a situation with no electricity but will take some time. After blended, add in the chocolate chips and pour into the pan. Bake for 30 minutes.

Let cool for at least 10 minutes.

NOTE
They will look a little under-cooked but they will firm up as they cool down.

Chickpea Cupcakes

INGREDIENTS
1 ½ cups semisweet chocolate chips
¼ cup vegetable oil
1 can chickpeas, drained
4 eggs
½ cup sugar
1 tsp baking powder
1 tsp vanilla extract

RECIPE
Preheat oven to 350° F. Grease a 12 muffin pan or line with paper baking cups.

Melt the chocolate chips and oil over simmering water, making sure to stir very frequently and to scrape down the sides to avoid scorching. Then blend the beans, eggs, sugar, baking powder and vanilla together in a food processor until smooth. Add chocolate mixture and blend again until smooth. Pour into muffin cups and bake for about 20 -25 minutes or until done.

NOTE
The blending can be done manually if you don't have electricity but will take more time to ensure a smooth mixture.

Chocolate Peanut Butter Dessert Hummus

INGREDIENTS
1 can chickpeas, drained and rinsed
¼ cup unsweetened cocoa powder
⅓ cup peanut butter
3 tbsp maple syrup or honey
¼ tsp ground cinnamon
¼ tsp salt
2 tsp pure vanilla extract
2 – 4 tbsp milk (can be cow, almond, rice, oat milk)

RECIPE
Add all ingredients, except milk, to a food processor and blend until smooth. Add 1 tablespoon of milk at a time until it has reached the desired consistency.

Serve with crackers, fruit, pretzels or something else yummy.

Bean Meringues

INGREDIENTS
½ cup of the liquid from a can of chickpeas
¼ tsp cream of tartar
¾ cup sugar
½ tsp vanilla extract

RECIPE
Preheat oven to 210° F and line a baking sheet with parchment paper.

Add the bean liquid and the cream of tartar to a bowl, then beat until soft peaks form. Gradually add in 1 tablespoon of sugar at a time, then continue beating. After beating for about 20 minutes, glossy peaks will start to form. Then you will beat in the vanilla extract.

Pipe mixture onto the parchment paper in small circles about 1 inch in diameter, leaving space in between each meringue. Then bake for about 90 minutes or until meringues are firm. Let cool completely.

Rice Pudding

INGREDIENTS
1 ½ cups cooked rice
2 cups milk
¼ teaspoon salt
⅔ cup raisins
1 egg beaten
⅓ cup sugar
1 tbsp butter
½ tsp pure vanilla extract

RECIPE
Add rice, 1 ½ cups milk and salt in a pan over medium heat. Cook for about 20 minutes until thick and creamy. Stir in remaining milk, raisins, beaten egg and sugar. Stir continually until egg is set which should be about 2 – 3 minutes. Remove from heat, then add butter and sugar.

VARIATIONS
You can add a lot of different things to this to change it up: coconut, chocolate chips, cinnamon, pumpkin spice or fruit. Give it a try!

Fried Rice Fritter

INGREDIENTS
1 cup flour
2 ½ tsp baking powder
1 tsp ground cinnamon
½ tsp salt
2 tsp pure vanilla extract
3 eggs
1 ½ cups cooked rice
Oil for frying
Powdered sugar for dusting
Syrup, honey, molasses or jam for dipping

RECIPE
Blend together the flour, baking powder, cinnamon and salt in a bowl, then set aside. Beat together the sugar, vanilla and eggs until thick and pale which should be about 4 – 5 minutes. Add the dry mixture and rice into the bowl, then stir just until blended. Cover the bowl and let it sit for about 30 minutes.

Pour about 2 inches of oil into a deep frying pan and heat it to about 360° F. Drop about 1 tablespoon of batter into the oil, working in batches. Make sure you leave room in the pan so the fritters don't stick to each other. Toss occasionally until golden brown. Use a slotted spoon to remove fritters when down and place on paper towel to drain. Dust with powdered sugar while still hot. Repeat until all batter is done.

Serve with syrup, honey, molasses or jam. Or just by themselves, they're yummy either way.

NOTE
Use a metal utensil to drop batter balls into oil and dip the utensil into the oil first so that the batter will slide off.

Sweet Tamales

INGREDIENTS
3 cups white rice, uncooked
2 cups plus 3 tbsp water
20 corn husks
8 oz cream cheese, softened
⅓ cup plus 2 tbsp powdered sugar
2 cups blueberries (or your favorite fruit)
½ cup lard at room temperature
Kitchen twine

RECIPE
Add uncooked rice and 2 cups water to a bowl and let soak for 4 hours, then drain. While you wait, soak the corn husks in warm water for about an hour or until they soften.

Add 2 tablespoons of powdered sugar to the cream cheese and mash together. Once the mixture is blended well, add 1 cup of blueberries and set aside.

Place ⅓ cup of rice mixture in the center of a husk and press to spread around. Add 1 ½ teaspoons of cream cheese mixture on top of the rice. Wrap tamales by folding the husk sides inward and then use the kitchen twine to tie both ends. Repeat until all ingredients are used.

Steam the tamales for about 1 ½ hours or until firm. Serve with additional fruit on top.

VARIATIONS
You could use your favorite jam or pie filling instead of the fresh fruit and cream cheese.

Puffed Rice

INGREDIENTS
1 ½ cups cooked rice
Oil for frying

RECIPE
Preheat oven to 250° F and line a baking sheet with parchment paper.

Place cooked rice on baking sheet and bake for about 2 - 2 ½ hours. When the rice is dry and all the moisture has evaporated, remove from oven and let cool completely.

Pour 2 inches of oil into large pot and heat to about 425° F. Drop in a few grains of rice to test the oil. If the rice starts to puff instantly, then the oil is ready.

Carefully add the rice to the oil, a little at a time, and fry for 3 – 6 seconds. Remove rice from oil using a metal sieve and place on paper towel to drain. Repeat until all the rice is puffed. Let cool completely and then use them in your favorite rice crispy recipe.

Rice Crepes

INGREDIENTS
1 ½ cups rice flour
3 eggs
¼ tsp salt
1 ¾ cups milk
2 tbsp canola oil
2 tbsp melted butter

RECIPE
Blend flour, salt, eggs, milk and butter until smooth. Then let the batter sit for about 30 minutes. It should have the same consistency as thick cream.

Heat a non-stick skillet over medium heat and brush lightly with oil. Pour ¼ cup batter in the pan and spread around. Cook on each side for about 60 – 90 seconds or until set. Repeat with remaining batter and remember to oil the pan before the next crepe.

Top with your favorite crepe topping!

Cinnamon Beans and Rice

INGREDIENTS
1 cup white rice, uncooked
2 cups water
½ stick butter
1 can chickpeas (garbanzo beans), drained and rinsed
1 tsp cinnamon
1 tsp vegetable oil
½ tsp maple syrup
¼ tsp salt

RECIPE
Preheat oven to 425 F.

Add chickpeas, 1 teaspoon cinnamon, 1 teaspoon oil, ½ teaspoon maple syrup and ¼ teaspoon salt in a bowl, then toss until evenly coated. Spread beans evenly on a baking pan in a single layer. Bake about 15 minutes or until the beans are crispy.

Meanwhile, add the rice, 2 cups of water and a little bit of butter to a pot. Cover and cook over medium-high heat until it starts to boil. Reduce heat to low and simmer for about 20 minutes or until rice is fully cooked. Immediately remove from heat and add ½ stick of butter. Once butter has melted, stir well.

Serve beans over rice and enjoy!

VARIATIONS
You can add a little extra sweetness by sprinkling sugar and cinnamon over the top before serving. Also, try adding some dried fruit to the bowl or replacing the cinnamon with pumpkin spice.

Sweet Buns

INGREDIENTS
1 cup dried red kidney beans
2 tbsp white sugar (for filling)
2 tbsp brown sugar
⅓ cup butter softened
2 cups water
1 cup rice flour
1 ½ tbsp white sugar (for buns)
½ cup boiling water
1 tbsp vegetable oil

RECIPE
Filling
Soak beans over night and cook until tender. Drain the water from the pot. Then add both sugars and butter. Use a potato masher to mash up the beans. The mixture should be just a little chunky but mostly mashed.

Turn the heat back on to medium-high. Stir and flip the mixture consistently to avoid burning. Continue until it becomes dark and holds its shape. Then remove from pan to cool. Once cool, use 1 cup of paste for this recipe. Divide the 1 cup of bean paste into 6 equal parts.

Buns
Add rice flour and 1 ½ tablespoons of white sugar in a bowl, then mix well. Pour ½ cup boiling water into the mixture and stir with a spoon.

While the dough is still warm, knead for a few minutes. Add 1 tablespoon of oil into the dough and continue to knead until it is no longer sticky. Roughly divide the dough into 6 pieces. Roll each piece into a ball and then flatten the dough. Keep the center thicker than the edges. Place the bean paste in the middle and roll into a ball. Repeat until all 6 are done, then use your palm to flatten the balls a little. Lightly grease a pan and heat over low. Once the pan is warmed, add the buns, cover and fry for about 5 minutes on each side or until done.

NOTE
You can experiment with the amount of sugar and butter in the filling to get the right amount of sweetness you like best. I prefer using less white sugar and more brown sugar myself.

Bean Custard Pie

INGREDIENTS
1 pie crust (see rice flour pie crust recipe)
6 oz evaporated milk
1 can navy beans, rinsed and drained
1/4 cup butter, melted
½ tsp cinnamon
½ tsp grated nutmeg
1 tbsp rice flour (or regular if you prefer)
1 ¼ cups sugar
1 tbsp vanilla extract
1 egg
1 egg yolk

RECIPE
Preheat oven to 450° F and place crust in pie pan.

Combine all the ingredients into a bowl and mash until smooth. Or place all ingredients into a food processor and blend until smooth. It takes longer to do by hand but it's possible if you don't have electricity or a food processor.

Pour into pie pan and bake for 15 minutes. Reduce heat to 350° F and bake for about 30 minutes or until the filling is set. Cool completely before slicing.

NOTES

NOTES

NOTES

NOTES

110   SNACKS

Snacks

Black Bean Crackers

INGREDIENTS
½ cup black bean flour
½ – ⅔ cup water
Salt to taste

RECIPE
Preheat oven to 350° F and grease a baking sheet.

Combine the salt and flour together. Slowly mix in the oil to form a sandy mixture. Then add half of the water and mix well. Continue to mix in more water until the batter is slightly runny. (And I mean just barely).

Pour a teaspoon of batter onto the baking sheet and use a fork to press the batter thin. Repeat until all the batter is used, remembering to leave plenty of space between each chip.

Bake for about 10 minutes, then flip and bake for an additional 10 minutes. Keep a close watch after you flip them so they don't burn.

VARIATIONS
Sprinkle with Cajun seasoning or a different one you like before baking.

Black Bean Dip

INGREDIENTS
2 cans black beans, rinsed and drained
½ cup onion, diced
1 garlic clove, minced
¼ tsp ground cumin
¼ tsp chili powder
½ tsp salt
¼ tsp pepper

RECIPE
Another easy recipe here, just put all the ingredients into a food processor and blend until smooth. Or you can mash by hand which will result in a chunkier dip.

VARIATIONS
Add cilantro, jalapeno and lime juice for a Tex-Mex flair. Or you could add some shredded cheese and serve warm.

Hummus

INGREDIENTS
1 can garbanzo beans
1 tbsp olive oil
1 tbsp lemon juice
1 garlic clove, crushed
½ tsp salt
2 drops sesame oil (optional)

RECIPE
Drain the beans and set the liquid aside. Blend beans and all other ingredients until smooth. Continue blending and slowly add in the bean liquid until you get the desired consistency.

VARIATIONS
There are lots of things you could add to change up the flavor. Some good ones are fire roasted tomatoes, cilantro, roasted bell peppers or pine nuts.

Rice Chips

INGREDIENTS
½ cup rice flour
¾ cup water
1 tbsp olive oil
Pepper
Salt

RECIPE
Preheat oven to 400° F and grease baking sheet.

Mix flour, water and oil together. Use a teaspoon to pour the batter onto the baking sheet. The batter will be runny and will spread a little. Wait until the batter has spread before you pour the next one so that you can leave room between each chip. Sprinkle the chips with salt and pepper.

Bake for about 6 minutes on each side.

VARIATIONS
Try different seasonings to find your favorite flavor. My favorite is salt and vinegar.

Garlic Rice Crackers

INGREDIENTS
1 cup rice flour
2 tbsp butter, melted
¼ cup water
1 tsp vegetable oil
½ tsp salt
½ tsp garlic powder
1 ½ tsp garlic paste

RECIPE
Preheat oven to 400° F and line a baking sheet with parchment paper.

Mix together the rice flour, 1 tablespoon melted butter, oil, salt, garlic powder and 1 teaspoon of the garlic paste. Slowly add in the water and mix until a dough forms. Knead the dough into a ball and place on the baking sheet. Place another sheet of parchment on top and then roll out the dough to about 1/8 inch thick. Using a sharp knife, cut the dough into squares. You don't need to spread the chips out after cutting them.

Mix the remaining melted butter and garlic paste, then brush on top of the crackers.

Bake for about 15 minutes or until the crackers are golden brown and crispy.

VARIATIONS
Make a sweet version by replacing the garlic with cinnamon and sugar before baking. Another option is to add cheese powder or other seasonings.

Rice Cakes

INGREDIENTS
2 cups cooked rice
2 tbsp flour
1 tbsp vegetable oil

RECIPE

Combine rice and flour in a bowl and knead until mixed well. Form the rice into small, flattened, rounded pieces. Warm oil in a skillet over low heat, then fry the rice cakes on each side for 2 – 3 minutes. Turn the heat up to high. Then fry again on each side until golden and crispy.

They taste great with fruit or jam for a sweet snack. They are also delicious with bean dip or salsa.

VARIATIONS

For a sweet version, add some sugar and cinnamon (or another sweet spice) to the rice when mixing. For a savory option, add some garlic or another seasoning to the mix.

SNACKS

NOTES

NOTES

NOTES

NOTES

DRINKS

Drinks

Sweet Rice Drink

INGREDIENTS
½ cup white rice, uncooked
1 ½ cups raw almonds
1 tsp ground cinnamon
⅓ cup sugar
2 cups boiling water
2 – 3 cups cold water
2 tsp vanilla
¼ tsp ground nutmeg

RECIPE
Blanch the almonds by bringing a pot of water to a boil and then adding the almonds. Boil for about 1 minute, then remove from heat and drain the water. Let the almonds cool down enough to handle. Remove the skins from the almonds by giving each one a little squeeze.

Place the almonds, rice, cinnamon, nutmeg and vanilla into a bowl with 2 cups of boiling water. Cover and let it sit overnight.

Add the sugar and the remaining water the next day. Then blend until smooth. Strain the liquid to remove any bits that haven't blended. Serve over ice.

Chocolate Rice Milk

INGREDIENTS
¾ cup white rice, uncooked
4 cups water
1 tsp vanilla extract
2 whole dates, pitted
2 tbsp cocoa powder

RECIPE
Soak the rice in 2 cups of very hot, but not boiling, water for about 2 hours. Add the remaining ingredients to the rice and blend until smooth. Taste to test the sweetness. You can add more dates or maple syrup, if you prefer, to increase the sweetness. Strain the liquid and serve cold.

VARIATIONS
Replace the dates with 2 tablespoons of maple syrup. Also, you can replace the chocolate with fresh berries.

Rice Wine

INGREDIENTS
½ cup white rice, uncooked
½ cup raisins
1 tsp yeast
8 ½ cups water
5 cups sugar

RECIPE
Rinse the rice and raisins very well. Pour the water into a pot and heat until it starts to boil. Once it starts to boil, turn the heat off and add in the rice and raisins. Let it sit until the mixture has cooled but is still warm. Pour the mixture into a glass jar with all of the other ingredients. Stir the mixture until it is mixed well and then place a lid on the jar.

Let the mixture sit. Every day you will stir it once in the morning and once in the evening for about 3 weeks. When the mixture stops bubbling, it's time to strain it. Strain the mixture through a fine cloth and discard the solids. Wash and dry the jar, then return the liquid to the jar. Let it sit for about a week, then it's ready to enjoy.

NOTE
You can further ferment rice wine to turn it into vinegar.

NOTES

MISCELLANEOUS

NOTES

Miscellaneous

Instant Rice

INGREDIENTS
2 cups white rice, uncooked
4 cups water

You will need a food dehydrator for this recipe.

RECIPE
Add water and rice to a pot. Cover and cook over medium-high heat until it starts to boil. Reduce heat to low and simmer for about 20 minutes or until rice is fully cooked.

Spread the hot rice on the dehydrator trays in a single layer. Dehydrate the rice at 135° F for around 5 – 8 hours. The timing will depend on a variety of factors. You will want to stir the rice a few times as it dries to break up any clumps. If left in clumps, it will not dry evenly.

Once the rice is completely dried and cooled, store in an airtight container. To cook instant rice just add equal parts water and rice, then boil for 5 – 10 minutes.

NOTE
For long term storage, instant rice can keep for a minimum of 2 – 3 years if packaged properly. Just make sure to seal it in mylar bags with oxygen absorbers.

Rice Syrup

INGREDIENTS
5 cups white rice, uncooked
2 cups barley malt powder
13 cups water

This recipe will make about 3 ½ – 4 cups of syrup.

RECIPE
Rinse rice with cold water several times until the water is almost clear. Place the rice and 5 cups of water into a large pot. Cover the pot and cook over medium heat for about 12 minutes. Reduce the heat to low, stir well, replace cover and simmer for about 10 minutes until the rice is cooked.

Turn off the heat and stir the rice. If there are some crunchy pieces at the bottom this is okay. Immediately add 8 cups of cold water and the 2 cups of barley malt powder. Mix well and replace the lid.

Let it sit for 1 hour. Then turn the heat to medium for 3 minutes. Stir it a few times and then turn the heat off. Repeat this process for a total of 6 hours. The mixture needs to stay between 100° F and 140° F for the entire 6 hours. As long as the pot is not sitting in a cool drafty environment, then following the above steps should ensure that it stays the right temperature.

Line a large strainer with cheese cloth and strain the mixture. Do this in smaller batches, making sure to squeeze the mixture. You want to get all of the liquid out. Throw away the solids (or use as compost). Pour the liquid into a large pot and turn the heat up to medium-high. Cook for about 1 ½ hours on a low boil. Stir occasionally.

It is done when the syrup becomes thick and runs off a spoon in a steady stream similar to maple syrup. Be careful that you don't cook it for too long as it will turn into a hard candy.

Once cooled, transfer to a glass jar.

Rice syrup can be used as a substitute for honey, corn syrup, maple syrup or molasses. It's not always a 1:1 ratio though, so keep that in mind.

NOTE
Barley malt powder is not a common ingredient to have on hand but is fairly easy to make. It has been included as a bonus recipe.

Rice Syrup Toffee

INGREDIENTS
1 cup rice syrup (see rice syrup recipe)
1 cup unsalted butter
¾ cup chopped almonds (optional)
6 oz dark chocolate (optional)

RECIPE
Line an 8" x 8" pan with foil and grease the foil.

Heat butter in a pot over medium heat until melted. Pour in the rice syrup and place a candy thermometer in the pot. Turn up the heat to medium-high, stirring constantly until the temperature reaches 270° F.

Turn the heat off and mix in ½ cup of the almonds. Pour the mixture into the lined pan and let it cool.

Melt the chocolate and pour over the toffee, then sprinkle the remaining almonds on top. Once the toffee has cooled completely, break it into pieces.

Hard Candy

INGREDIENTS
2 ¾ cups rice syrup
1 ⅓ cups sugar
¼ tsp food coloring (optional)
15 drops flavored oil

RECIPE
Combine syrup, sugar and food coloring in a pot and cook over low heat until the sugar is dissolved. When bubbles start to appear, insert candy thermometer. Continue to cook until the temperature reaches 300° F, then remove from heat. Stir in the flavored oil.

Pour the mixture into a lightly greased baking sheet. After it has cooled for about 5 – 10 minutes, you can use a knife to score the candy. This will make breaking it easier but is not necessary. After it has cooled completely, break apart and enjoy.

VARIATIONS
Adding the food coloring is optional but adds a nice touch and can be used to distinguish flavors. Some flavors to try are peppermint, orange, cinnamon, spearmint and many more. You could also pour the mixture into candy or lollipop molds if you have them.

Bonus Recipe: Barley Malt Powder

INGREDIENTS
Barley grains

RECIPE
Rinse and drain the grains very well. Then place the grains in a jar and fill with water to several inches above the grains. Let them soak for about 12 hours.

Drain and rinse the grains again. Then cover the jar and place it in a spot that is out of direct sunlight.

You will continue to drain and rinse the grains twice a day until they are ready. Once the sprout is the same length as the grain, then they are ready. Rinse and drain one last time.

Spread the grains out on a baking sheet and dry with low heat. The ideal temperature is around 100° F and should not exceed 135° F which will kill the enzymes. Make sure to stir them a few time so they dry evenly. When they are hard and completely dry they are ready for the next step. Finally, grind them into a fine powder.

USING BARLEY MALT POWDER
What can you do with barley malt powder? Other than make rice syrup you can add it to baked goods to improve the flavor and texture, use it for malt shakes, make a chocolate malted drink mix (very similar to a popular brand a lot of you probably drank as a kid) and so much more.

NOTES

NOTES

NOTES

NOTES

NOTES

Note from the Author

Dear Reader,

I believe that everyone should be prepared for anything that may come. So, I hope that you have gained some valuable knowledge with this book. If so, reach out and let me know. You can find me on Facebook at:

www.facebook.com/jmmason13

Occasionally, I send out an email with important information about survival tips, preparedness and new books. If you would like to be included in that email just head on over to www.survivalzulu.com and click the newsletter link.

Also, consider helping me to reach more people. The best way for you to do that is to leave a review.

JM Mason

Printed in Great Britain
by Amazon